SCENE

SCENE

BY

E. GORDON CRAIG

With a Foreword and an Introductory Poem

BY

JOHN MASEFIELD

Benjamin Blom
New York

First published by
The Oxford University Press, 1923
Reissued 1968,
by Benjamin Blom, Inc. Bx 10452

Library of Congress Catalog Card No. 65-20498

Manufactured in the United States of America

FOREWORD

LAST summer there was held in London an exhibition of designs, scenes and models made by the artists of the theatres of the world. The exhibition showed the mind of the world. To look at those works was to see how the brain wrought in each country.

To workers in the theatre here in England the exhibition was cheering, because the cry 'of our decadence in the theatre', at that time loudly raised, was answered by it. The designs, scenes, and models made by Englishmen were among the best in the exhibition. The very best of them, which persist in the mind months after the exhibition has been closed, were by Mr. Gordon Craig, the writer of this book.

The purpose of the book is to display some of Mr. Craig's work and method, in its relation to the theatres of the past, and to suggest what it might do in the theatre of to-day if employed.

Mr. Craig needs no word of introduction. As an artist and thinker for the theatre, he is known where theatres are: as a writer, he is known where good English is read. All that the writer of a preface can do for him is to say how good a thing it would be if his work could be used in an English theatre.

For a great many years there has been a feeling that our theatre is defective. Some have felt that our speaking is bad, others that our lighting is bad, or our scenery vulgar; others that our plays are not 'serious' enough, or not 'intense' enough, or too intense, or that they 'prove nothing', or try to prove too much, or are not full enough of the reform of an institution or the immorality of a type of citizen; or not literary enough, not poetical enough, or (more frequently) 'not red-blooded

(vii)

enough'. Some claim that our acting is not based upon tradition nor trained by persistent and varied hard work; others that the fault is his or the error hers. Most have felt that something is and has been amiss, though they have continued to support the faulty institution, and to amend it here and there.

Probably the defects of an institution are due to one cause: that it has ceased to attract and to employ the finest types of intellect. Most of the defects of our stage to-day are due to this cause. It has not employed the finest intellects of the last century. It is not now employing the best designs, minds, and imaginations of workers for the theatre now living. The Exhibition of last summer proved that England has noble imaginations in her theatre, but her theatre at present is not using them. 'What universal genius, and what a want of method', as Goethe said of us, a hundred years ago, in a time not unlike this.

Twenty years ago I belonged to a little company of actors and writers who wished to found a new kind of theatre in London. We had in mind a small theatre where nothing should be played that was not a masterpiece of the theatre, whether tragical, romantic, or merry, by one of the master-playwrights of the world. As there are galleries set apart for the works of master-painters and sculptors, and concert-halls reserved for the playing of none but the choice musicians, so, we felt, there should be a theatre reserved for the works of the master-playwrights, whose beauty, majesty, or mirth of mind ranks them with the greatest of men. Our plan was stated with some force in a newspaper of the time. The writer of the statement pled our cause on these grounds: that in the London of that time no single masterpiece of the theatre was being played; that this could not be said of any other capital in Europe, and that he felt sure that there must be enough people in London, fond of the masterpieces of the theatre, to support such a little theatre as we hoped to establish.

The scheme came to nothing, for this very good reason, that the man for it was not among us. I mention it here only for this further very good reason, that the pleas of that stater of our cause are as true to-day as they were twenty years ago.

In the list of plays now being performed in London there is but one play which can be called a masterpiece of the theatre, and that play beautiful as it is, is being performed in a little theatre, in a distant suburb. The great work of the theatre, whether tragical, romantic or merry, is still either not performed here or is performed with insufficient means.

The theatre, as it exists in London to-day, is crushed by ground rents, sub-lettings, speculation, and by the lack of subsidy, from either the State or the rich man with a sense of style. It cannot afford to perform the masterpieces of the theatre. The nation, with her mind changed profoundly by the war, turns to all master-thought for daily bread. As she cannot find master-thought in the theatre, she turns to recreate the theatre. All over England there are little bodies of men and women making theatres for themselves. In those theatres the masterpieces of the theatre are being played, if not well, at least sincerely, with delight both to the actor and the audience. England makes for herself what her institutions do not provide. The time is ripe for the State, or better, some rich man with a sense of style, to build and endow a new theatre for this new England, so that the new thought in the theatre may have a home. What greater glory can a man have than to build that which will be the home of knowledge, beauty, and mirth for centuries to come? What do people do with their wealth? What use of wealth gives us pleasure where we go? Our churches, colleges, schools, and old foundations, our roads and bridges, all, once, the gifts of piety and humanity. This most beautiful race deserves the utmost from her lucky ones. Will not one among her lucky ones give to Mr. Craig, a noble and disciplined artist, son of a beloved artist, the means to use what his long toil has perfected?

ONCE we were masters of the arts of men,
  Poetry, music, painting, building, all
Beautiful noble arts were ours then,
  Decking this England as for festival.

A son of England could not lift his head
  Then without knowing rapture of delight.
The English hedgerow rose of beauty shed
  Into all English hearts its red and white.

Our current coins bore then the sacred stamp
  Of style in the used thing.   In the world's tower
In space's darkness, England was a lamp.
  Her lovely brain beheld; her hand had power.

In these two things alone, her spirit shows
Her Saint was then Saint George, her mark, a rose.

* * *

Builded in every village in the land,
  Cut in the lasting stonework, you will find
Marvellous relics that an English hand
  Left as the tokens of an English mind.

Their spires (rough stone translated) lift aloft,
  Their gargoyles grin, their bells, in belfries dark,
Still dole the time by hours to the croft,
  Columns still bear the towers and are stark.

Over all England beauty was like June
  Deep in men's spirits, when we made these things,
Nightingales, dew, the dog-rose and the moon,
  Beauty of queens, authority of kings,

And faith of men, all merged, that centuries on
Eternal things should shine as then they shone.

* * *

I saw the work of all the world displayed,
    The thinkers of the theatres of earth
Sent, to be shown, the utmost they had made,
    Much of it mad, much pleasant, some of worth.

But, worthiest of it all, this English man's
    Stood out supreme, as, in a paling sky,
When stars go out, the morning planet scans
    Our twilit world with an untroubled eye.

There the work stood for England, and made mute
    Our enemies who mocked us with decay;
There was a life's devotion come to fruit,
    Enduring beauty keeping death at bay.

Here is the work.   Who, greater than his age,
Will use this work to consecrate the stage?

* * *

I cannot tell who will, but inly know
    That faithful work was never yet forlorn.
The best abides, the lusts and fashions go,
    Time and the grasses cover over scorn.

By unexpected ways despaired—of things
    Come into being after hope has ceast.
Over our fainting shoulders there are wings,
    By unseen hands our harvest is increast.

Here in our darkness now the powers of light
    Stir us to change this land that we have filled
With squalor and with nightmare and with night.
    To Beauty's self; they summon to rebuild,

Rebuild in beauty on the burnt-out coals,
Not to the heart's desire, but the soul's.

JOHN MASEFIELD.

(xi)

SCENE

Art employs its material not to disguise thoughts but to express them.

(1) ¶ Words having lost so much of their meaning—six different words often meaning the same thing—one word at times meaning six different things—it is only natural that this world should have come to accept as true the saying which went the rounds of the eighteenth century, and which Voltaire polished into 'ils n'emploient les paroles que pour déguiser leurs pensées'.

The world could not help it—speech was always a too pretty, too facile, little thing—and even babies use it straightway to lie with . . . and a word is believed.

But nor babies nor wise men can lie quite so easily or prettily with gestures.—The little animal may have long ago mastered this subtlety . . . nature is always a delight and a surprise . . . but man not yet.

To man words come easiest and earliest to lie with.—So that now in this twentieth century nearly all speech is a lie.—I would not go so far as to laughingly admit that speech of that kind was an art. I should rather call it a mess.

Once a merely natural thing—it became an art; but when it exceeded its natural term of life, having talked itself hoarse—black in the face—the silver of speech rubbed off and we came to the lead underneath, and inside the lead . . . lies.

*   *   *

So that now, when all I wish to speak of to you is about those things which we put on the stage of a Theatre to stand for *the Place*[1] in which a Drama is supposed to be happening, I find myself held up for lack of the right word by which to describe it so that every one shall understand above all else what I do not mean.

If I use one of the several words three of you will take me to mean one thing, three of you another, and three more . . . but I grow too hopeful,—surely nine will not read this book.

For while, alas, it may be true that we write and utter words merely to disguise our thoughts—we still read them precisely for the other reason, which is to learn of things we have not seen, to hear of things we have not heard of, from those who have heard and have seen.

---

[1] 'A nice place' said a dear old friend to me on looking at the model of the scene I shall describe later—and I have always thought this was the best word to use—far better than scene—it is a place if it seem real—it is a scene if it seem false.

That is why we read unless we are funny little men, too early bitten—crying too soon; ancient little men—wishing to be masters of their surroundings—of themselves—of life—of nature—unable to be any such thing, but oh how persuaded (for that aged air tells it as clearly as a train's shrill whistle, 'we are going through a tunnel') . . . persuaded that all life is but ashes . . . man a mule or a swine, woman a cat or a hen, and the first ruling law of human nature the desire to eat.

But six men and women, say three of each, will read what I am now writing and hear something which is undisguised. So for these six I will try. But then they must be content—it is only a small matter that we shall speak of—the larger matter lies in the Designs . . . and these must speak for themselves, for I shall not speak of them.

* * *

(2) ¶ *The Place* in which a drama is supposed to be happening before your eyes may be Athens 100 B.C. or a street in Athens 400 B.C., Rome A.D. 100 or one room in Rome A.D. 456; it may be Rome to-day, 1922.

Or it may be a ship's cabin at sea—in port—a canal in Venice—a heath in Yorkshire;—or it may be a publisher's office—or a church at Oxford—a house on the hills along Yang-Tsé-Kiang, a forest of cedars by Pisa—some room in Rue de Bagnolet in 1752 . . . a thousand thousand different places!

It may be any place known to you or to me or heard of:—it may be even those places off the earth,—as, for example, in Goethe's 'Faust',—in Byron's 'Manfred', in Shakespeare's 'Tempest'. It may be a slum—a palace—or Heaven or Hell,—though of course here we must be very careful lest we offend the sceptical.

¶ And we have given a name to this Place—and here begins the trouble: for it seems that one name was not enough, and so we have given it several names—and confusion lays another wreath on the tomb of order. Confusion is always laying these wreaths:—what a spectre . . . with ironical gesture and grin, . . . quite like death itself.
We have called this Place, Scene—Scenery—Décors—Decorations.
All these words seem to me, and perhaps to you, to squabble.
This confusion arose because different people had different notions of what *Drama* was and wanted a change.

We have to look into these changes for a moment: it must be rapidly spoken as is an argument to an old play.

(2)

THE ARGUMENT.

1st Drama.   Classical (Greek or Roman).   The Pagan.

> One place—one time—one action.
>
> (Unity of *place*, time, and action—not of *scene*, time, and action.)

Open air : vast theatres : The same Drama is for the People and for the Few.   It is Sacred or Profane—Tragedy or Comedy—no ' comfortable ' Drama.

Dance—Song—Speech—Masks—Architecture combine in this Drama.   Greatly planned—deliberate.

The language used is that which can be understood by all in the Theatre.

It overruns the whole known world.

2nd Drama.   The Medieval.   The Christian.

> Unity of place, time, and action gone.

This Drama generally shown in churches.

Sacred and profane coming to be mixed.

Still no ' comfortable ' Drama.

The same elements—Dance—Song—Speech—Masks and Architecture combine to create it.   Greatly planned—deliberate.

The language used is that which cannot be understood by the uneducated masses who throng the building.

It dominates Europe.

3rd Drama.   Italian.   The Commedia dell' Arte.   Believing all things.

> The unities of place, time, and action return and are found valuable.
>
> This Drama performed in the streets.
>
> It is Profane—Grotesque Comedy.

Stillnot ' comfortable ' Drama.

The same elements go to making it—only all these are seized on spontaneously—nothing deliberate—little planned—improvisation.

The language of the common people used.

It spreads like fire over Europe.

4th Drama.   ——————————————— ?   Believing nothing.

> The 3rd Drama become fixed—settling down—becoming ' comfortable '.

The same elements as before, except the Architecture—painted scenes in place of this.

Indoors.

Artificial light for the first time.

(3)

(3) ¶ And with change of Drama came change of scene.   Change in Drama had come because of climate.

Drama had gone indoors in the cold season—and so impatient was man to be always amusing himself in the wrong season that he could not wait for the warm season to arrive.   The error was not the artist's error—it was due to bad government.

¶ Drama, they say,—and it is easily to be believed—sprang from some spontaneous leapings and laughings during the brilliant months of the southern year.

It is to be believed because there is some sense in an ecstasy at such a time, in the open air, and a wish to do something, sing and dance something, before the Gods to whom at that time they attributed all these blessings of warmth, gay hearts—loving friends—victory over enemies— the water! . . . the water! . . . the sun and sky and the cooling nights . . . the wine! . . . the corn . . . and abundance.

To sit egoistically writing their memoirs to explain to a public that the corn, wine, water and all were merely the result of their own particular foresight and energy never occurred to these free men our fathers—to them it was a God or two who had done it all.—Praise, then, and laughter before the God.

(Now think for a moment of Strindberg—of Becque—of Shaw or any other modern! Are these or are these not an advance on the older men ?—

These *wait* on the people : arguing with them—patting them on the back—hob-nobbing dramatists, but our forefathers led the people.)

So then the scene of these earliest Dramas was put up in the open air—

Made of that tough stuff which alone is able victoriously to compete with the sun, the wind, the rain, and the teeth of time, . . . Stone.

¶ The whole Theatre was of stone—*the whole Theatre was the Scene*. One part of it held spectators, the other actors; but all of it was Scene— the Place for the Drama.[1]

Division betwixt performer and spectator was not to be insisted on— it was to be observed mutually—mutely.

There was no curtain :—The place called *Skene* (scene) was the place farthest from the spectators—and this was the back wall of the whole Place or Theatre.

---

[1] 'A Greek town could hardly be so small or so remote as not to have its own Theatre and dramatic festival.'   (Flickinger.)

The actors did not slide in and slide out along this wall as though they were flat and on their own inimitable vases: they did not come on like white mice in a silent room, unseen, unheard; they came on and forward straight for the spectators—into the very centre of them—near them— singing—leaping—gliding—realizing the three dimensions of the place.

¶ Their *skene* then was really Scene for the first, and (I think) for the last time in the History of the World.

—not scenery—not décors. Stone, white—red—yellow—brown— black—blue—green, ... who knows what colour;' for colour cannot have been forgotten by the Greeks: but it was not colour brought in by the pailful,—brought in by some studio-painter out of work, for the Greek painters were always employed in Greece, always in their place ... outside the Theatre.

¶ Their Scene then was a *genuine* thing. A work of architecture. Un- alterable except for trifling pieces here and there,—except for the everlasting change which passed from morn till morn across its face as the sun and moon passed.

Their Drama was triumphant ... without contortions it passed away triumphantly.

(4) ¶ The next scene which appears in Europe is also an architectural one— for the next drama was also a religious one, and, being young in heart at that time, we Europeans had that old zest to do things properly.

This old notion of doing the thing properly seems to have always dominated us so long as we had some one or something outside ourselves to do it for.

A god—that was a reality for which we could lose self-conscious- ness—throwing our egoisms out of us, we were in a fit state to do some- thing worth while.

That state seems to me to be the only state in which really great art can be achieved by a man or by a nation. Much talk to-day about Communal art! Very fine and very possible—but not while you Com- munists remain self-conscious—and are more in love with yourself than I am. But you know that ... I need not preach.

' Did you ever see the walls of the Church of St. Mark in Venice?
60 paces away from them they look as though hung with soft silk hangings of elaborate design.
Close to them one sees they are plain slabs of stone—but *what* stone—how selected—how cut—how joined.
The style is the miracle, not the stone.
Even so and, I do not doubt, even more wonderful was the *way* of the Greeks from whom Venice learnt all.

¶ This second architectural scene which appeared in Europe was the Church.

It was not merely a raised platform—a scene—at the end of a church :—it was *the whole church*.

This Church was Theatre and Stage. Place for spectators and for actors, and both spectators and actors united as worshippers—gay—excited—bursting with gratitude to something outside themselves.

Why go to church—why go to witness a Drama, whether tragic or gay, unless you go with speed as children come running to kiss?

I go no more to church nor to theatre, where such excitement is absent.

And yet I go to churches and to theatres.

¶ In this Church-Theatre which we Europeans made for Thanksgiving purposes all was very splendid—very costly : jewels, silver, and gold . . . a feast of it : music . . . a sea of it; troubled but triumphant still. Latin is spoken . . . no one understands except the *few*. All was genuine—still genuine—glowing with reality. All is still well with Drama and Scene.[1]

(5) ¶ The third scene which appeared in Europe was genuine too.

It was the plain wall of a street, or a cellar wall,—a loggia of a townhall, or some minor façade or wing of a palace.

All is still well with us. It is not revolution—it is a beginning. We have given in a little—but we have seized other chances open to us.

The *troubled* tones—movements—looks which had forced an entrance to our Drama in the last development of our Drama had come to be a strain on our nerves. We were growing peevish and troubled too. We did not forget the triumphant 'Tollite portas' . . . but we shuddered because . . . dare we say it . . . the bleeding face and torn body of the Son was too much—too many such faces and bodies were brought to

---

[1] I omit mention of the unnecessary theatres and scenes of this age which were conceived in desperation—an unnecessary despair which sprang from some fatal obstinacy, some revolt. These morality and 'mystery' stages were out of the Church—and out of place. The work done on them a kind of childish work—the vulgar speech howled or jabbered when fine Latin sung or chanted had been rejected by some revolutionaries in a not perfect Church, but a far more perfect Church than they ever were to find again . . . a far more perfect stage, scene—and Drama.

Mr. E. K. Chambers, whose first chapter in his second volume of 'The Mediaeval Stage' never fails to thrill me, barest history though it be, tells us clearly what this solemn gay Drama—stage and scene—was like. Since 1903, when his book first appeared in England, I have owed him a debt of gratitude which I repay by turning continually, at least three or four times a year, to his book and reading it. It is the finest English work on this theme that exists to-day.

us to see—all torn bodies, all drawn mouths,—all grief and pain—all—and the incense suffocated us, . . . the gloom was coming down on us.

We will go out—we try to find the door—we go out—we get out—fresh air—'thank God'.

And for a time we do without the old tragic play altogether: never mind it: let it be forgotten: . . . it was all too terrible to remember . . . it had been made too terrible to see. Nothing else—the thing itself, once so severe and noble and so severely treated thrilled us—but *cheapness* entered into the way of doing it . . . good-bye.

¶ And now sitting at our door in the sun one day we see over the way against the yellow-grey wall three strange figures—we peer at them with our eyes shaded. Are they not rather like . . . . no, that was only a terrible fancy, to be forgotten . . . let us go in.

Next day the same—and laughter too, and people watching too—and laughing. I go out.—I draw nearer. The same three strange figures leaping and gesticulating . . . not *really* at all like those images with the torn faces and the broken knees—and now I am nearer still I see how absurd my notion was . . . they are laughing all the time. Misery and agony does not laugh: . . . only the victorious laugh—yet till I sleep I seem to see the woebegone vision of a martyr.

¶ These are the new performers,—we the new, rather terrified, grinning spectators—our theatre the street—our scene the mound of earth in front of the yellow-grey wall—our seats . . . our own heels or a stone.

The Commedia dell' Arte was born.

(6) ¶ The Fourth Scene.

'We must do something, it seems,' cried the Duke on perceiving one afternoon his principal piazza crowded with all his retainers, his friends, his very family, 'and nothing to sit down on'—and all watching five great actors acting on a bare platform . . . 'we must really do something'; and he supplied the seats the next day. And up sprang the fourth scene on a handsome stage with a roof to it and all sorts of machinery and every possible protection afforded to Donna Bianca della Bella.

It cost the Duke all his spare time . . . and some millions of ducats . . . what of that: it must be well done, he said, or left alone. Very swagger!

¶ This fourth stage with its Scene was the acknowledgement made by the aristocracy of the existence of great actors—and was a present to the people.

A more magnificent scene would be inconceivable. Not noble like the Greek scene, not forbidding as the church scene became, not tragicomic like the street scene of the grotesque comedians in rags :—it was a positive, a deliberate improvisation, brilliant and full of faults. All the architects, painters, poets, and engineers were called in by the Duke from all parts of Italy,—and if he dwelt in France like Henry IV, then out of Italy ; if like Philip in Spain, then into Spain.

No sooner had the first Duke acted like a Duke than about six or seven more took to it;—then a Cardinal, a King or two,—then an Emperor. It went on spreading, this idea of doing things like a Duke, like a King, until every Court possessed one, two, or sometimes four theatres. As in Parma in 1690 when Duke Farnese had two theatres in his Palace, two in his Garden, and two in the Town, and between May 20 and 25 had performances in four of these.[1]

Doubting at all whether it was so very swagger, this fourth Scene, you only have to visit Parma to satisfy youself. It is nearly all there as it was. You have only to turn to the works by Serlio, Palladio, Arnaldi, Sirigatti, and their followers, to find the missing parts.

Italy gave us the third and fourth Stages and their Scene.

No longer was the idea of Durability uppermost with the inventors of it. The demand was for *Change*, and change was supplied.

—Change of place, and therefore change of scene. Change of time too. . . .

Bring the sea on our stages . . . the world . . . the stars and the winds . . .

Now change—presto—the underworld. . . . .

Now—the abodes of the Gods. . . .

Now the palace of Xuxiemes, Emperor of Troy . . .

Now the source of the river Tiber . . .

And no longer all seeming to take place in one day, or four hours. Cover six days or longer ;—let a year lapse between scenes—(Shakespeare).

¶ This fourth stage was generally built of wood. Sometimes the outer walls of the building would be of solid stone or brick, but inside all was often but of wood—of canvas—of destructible stuff. But so tenacious is an old virtue that the men of those days could not manage

---

[1] From May 20 to 25, Duke Ranuccio II presented four operas on the most lavish scale known in those days. One, ' Il Favore degli Dei ', was given at night on the stage of the Teatro Farnese in the Palace. This theatre seated 4,500 people, and exists to-day. The second opera was given by day on a stage built over a large basin of water called ' la Grande Peschiera '. The spectators sat in a specially constructed theatre—ten thousand were present—' La Gloria d'Amore ' was performed. The other two operas were ' L'Età dell' Oro ' and ' L'Idea di Tutte le Perfezioni '— these being performed in the Teatrino Farnese. This small theatre held 2,000 spectators.

to avoid making their flimsiest things far stronger and more durable than our best attempts.

Of course the Shakespearian Stage and Scene are unique—not related to this 4th stage or its scene. The Elizabethan playhouse was the work of a builder who was very practical—very thorough. There had been no time or opportunity for English architects to turn to the matter of Theatre designing as in Italy, and so Shakespeare, arriving with all his suddenness, found no real Theatre such as we should have liked to prepare for him had he only given us a little notice.

Had an English architect turned his attention to this work during Shakespeare's life, or shortly after his death, we should probably have now some building as noble as those built in Italy by Palladio, Alliotti, and Scamozzi, and a building which would have been a guide to us now as to how Shakespeare wished his plays performed. For there was John Thynne, and there was John Shute, living—either of these were well able, one would imagine, to conceive and carry out the building of a theatre—or, failing these, Robert Adams or John Smithson: Inigo Jones too. We had the architects, but gave the work to builders who made us an excellent, but unremarkable, construction in wood, somewhat like an inn-yard or a bear-pit—by no means inadequate, but also in no way worthy of the peculiarly unique drama of which we had just come into possession.

'A public authority meanly housed may be meanly esteemed', said our Sovereign lately, when speaking on the subject of architecture and its relation to civic life, and Shakespeare's drama has come to be even less than meanly esteemed to-day by—the public.

Doubtless the simple, fine mind of the scholar may find in the mud hut of the primitive man a better habitation for a noble man or a noble thought than is a palace built of more precious material by a Bramante or a Palladio.

Possibly these palaces of Italy, and the Indian temples, the Parthenon, and the Theatre of Dionysus, are not simple enough to the great minds.

Indeed it would be a delight to find some English master conceiving a yet simpler, a yet nobler, building for our Shakespearian Drama.

At Durham, Lincoln, and Canterbury our architects made shrines for our holy books—but for our human book no fitting house was made.

Exactly what kind of house this book asks for they who read should be able to decide—but to read 'Lear' and 'The Tempest' and still be tongue-tied is a pity.

Maybe if we listened to it more we should come to find the right measures, conceive proportions adequate, and create a form which for ever might challenge comparison with the noblest.

I do not know—I can only say that it is not possible to speak of

(9)

the insignificance of the stage and scene made in the sixteenth century for our great Englishman, and I must be excused if my constant love and reverence for our English Drama prejudices me in its favour to the extent of demanding for it the best theatre in Europe—and refusing to accept a makeshift.

And into this fourth theatre of the sixteenth century came Perspective in scene. *Perspective* had been lately discovered in Italy[1] by Uccello about 1450, or by his master or his master's master. Discovered then or not it was now in 1500–1550 become a trick much used and marvelled at on the stage . . . new to many, for only noticed by them now for the first time.

Scene makers seized on perspective as it lent itself to having a good game, and displayed it to right and to left, and kept up this game until only yesterday.

Now what made it so popular?—what prevented us all from hissing? —It was his Serenissimo the Duke.

In every theatre built in those days there was always one spot (and one only) from which every perspective scene seemed reasonable—a reality—perfect.

It was not a fixed spot . . . but it was a single one.

Having found this spot, the architect (who was also scenographer) so built his auditorium, so arranged his boxes, circles, seats, as to leave a clear space around that spot. On it he placed a dais, no matter where it might be;—this dais he drew forwards—or moved it back—until he had found the perfect spot from which to view the perspectives.

Once found, he, as it were, nailed the dais to the ground : placed one chair there for the Duke, . . . for the man who had made possible all these splendid festivals . . .

Perspective scenery, therefore, is due entirely to a proper and pleasant understanding of Authority.

In no other spot in the Theatre was it possible to obtain a perfectly just view :—the moment one moved off to the right, to the left, or forwards or backwards, the effect began to be rather strange :—move farther still, N. S. E. or W., and it looked decidedly odd : move still farther, and it looked excentric, and finally became ridiculous.

But such was the power of the idea of Royalty—and the personal power of the Ruler—and the innate courtesy of his subjects, that, while some might descend to think peevishly, as a whole the rest of the city had made up its mind that all was as it should be.

---

[1] Vasari states this, though I have seen plenty of a strangely Theatric Perspective in Pompeii: and when at Pompeii I thought I began dimly to see what a Roman Theatre and its stage and scene may have looked like.

It went the round: 'The Duke has never seen it as we see it—he gets a perfect view—' and explanations as to how this could be were given from artists to people, from masters to servants; toys even came out which proved the point . . . 'Hold the toy thus and you get the view the Duke gets.' Ah, he gets that view? they queried. He does! Then all is well.

They knew he would not complain: that was enough. They knew also that their different views were not his view; that from their seats all the architecture twisted—pillars—arches—steps—all went the wrong way: but they agreed that, provided the Duke was pleased, they would notice nothing, say nothing. So Italian, so witty—indifferent—great.

A potato—or a metranome—(and I know men like each), may possibly think it silly rather than great: these must continue to argue it out with the human race, for my notion of happiness is not that of a potato or a machine. I enjoy to see another enjoy, provided I am fond of the other. Unless the Duke is really enjoying himself at this theatre of his which we have made, I and my friends are not happy. You, potato, and you, machine,—you *are*:—meno male!

¶ And for some centuries every one was content.

And, indeed, if Architects and Dukes had remained what they were, then perhaps the perspective scene would have not become what it became twenty years ago.

But about the year 1789 some trouble in Paris began to affect the eyesight of the Europeans—and now good perspective scenery, that fourth scene, is practically no more.

I hear that the People are growing stronger year by year. I have never known exactly what that meant—not having noted much weakness in those People in Greece, Italy, Egypt, Rome, France, in the ancient days.

Still, if they are growing *stronger*, I find it difficult to resist the notion that they must at the same time become sweeter—and then they will be sure to remember that the last Theatre—with its Scene—was a present to them from the Duke—and they in their new-won strength will surely find the grace to present the whole Aristocracy with the next Theatre.

For, broadly speaking, there have been but four Theatres—four Scenes—four Dramas—in Europe.

The first was the best of all, but the last was ever so good . . . and the two in between immense.[1]

---

[1] It was in this Theatre of the Duke and for this fourth scene that machinery came to be employed:—not for the first time, for some machinery was used in the Greek Theatre and some in the Church. But their machines seem to have been

(7) ¶ I give you four small designs (Figs. 1, 2, 3, 4) which will show you these four stages side by side.'

Innumerable variations on these four themes exist in our Public and Private Collections of Books, Prints, and Drawings, and the student will, if he have patience, come in time to see some of them.

My purpose is not to go into this matter here as an Historian does— I have not his ability. My purpose is to keep your attention on these four designs, so that you may see the matter as a stage man sees it—a stage man of no narrow or particular school, but an ordinary stage man who has come to understand, after thirty years' practice and study of the stage, that each stage has its place, and that each stage, each scene, *in* its place is admirable—but *out* of its place merely nothing.

Bear this in mind, for it is surely true.

The stage has often offended; but after inquiry I find it has not offended more than painting, sculpture, music, architecture, and letters. All art, and each part of the art, when out of place, offends. Each example must be in its *right place*, appear at the *right time*, have reason for appearing at all, and all is well. . . .

---

brought in and taken away; they were not FIXTURES . . . whereas in the sixteenth and seventeenth centuries the machines became fixed.

Fixed machinery, which prevents the mobility of scene, must be a curse to Drama. It was used in the eighteenth century to facilitate things—to make changes of scene easier. It made them only more difficult. It so acted on our stage work that by 1800 we could change nothing . . . all became *repetition*. Wagner, who is supposed to have reformed it all, acted like all reformers . . . he accepted the thing as it was and made a few improvements.

Machinery still controlled the scene.

Alexander Hevesi has pointed out that the machinist is the enemy of the Theatre—he and the realist. We should come to realize the truth of this. There are other and better fields for the machinist. Art should exclude mechanism.

' The design which I give you of the *First* Scene is the best I could get—How best ?—because it shows the stage walls of stone—architectural.

Of course between the Greek and the Roman stages—which are two parts of this *First* Scene—there were differences, but they were differences mostly of elaboration. The essentials were the same—the *point*,—that this theatre was *all* of stone—was architectural—the 'Scene' was of a piece with the other two parts—'Orchestra' and 'Arena'.

Speaking of this 'Scene', Robustiano Gironi says in his 'Saggio intorno al Teatro dei Greci'—

—'. . . La scena dei Greci era *perfettamente simile* a quella dei Romani . . .'

It may have been or it may not have been '*perfettamente*' simile.

None can *swear* to it—not even the great German Dörpfeld—for no one seems to have come across a pure Greek Scene standing.

Therefore I give you this picture for the Classical scene 'par excellence'.

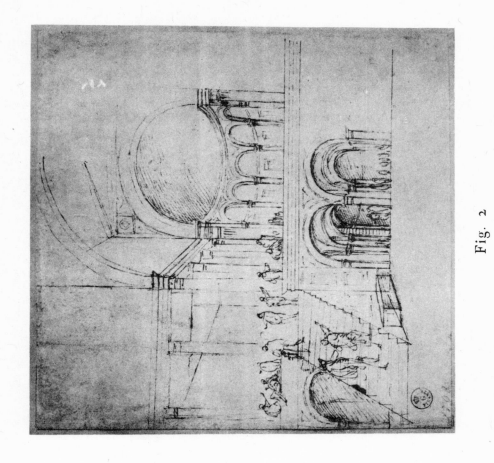

Fig. 2

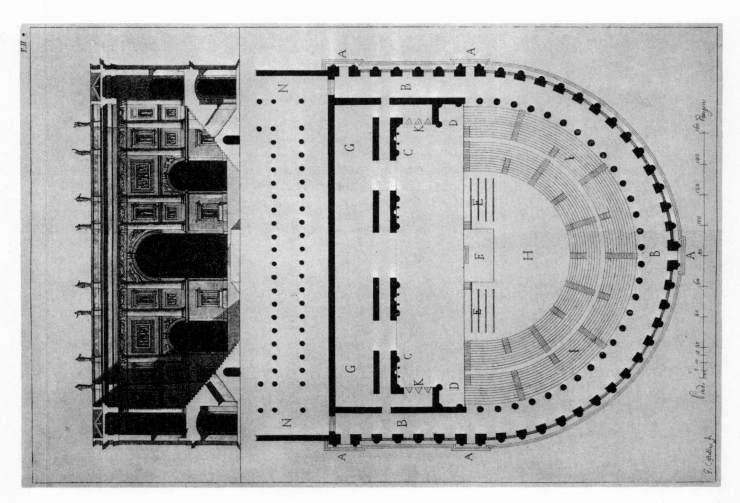

Fig. 1

Razullo   Cucurucu.

Fig. 3

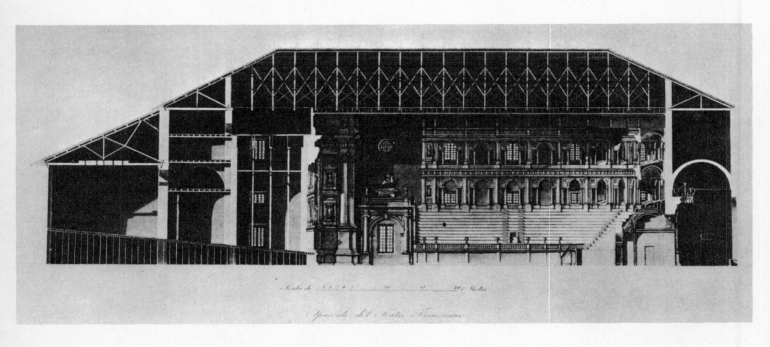

Fig. 4

And it should be the pleasure of all workers in the Dramatic Art to see to it that nothing is out of place . . . and no one out of place.

It should be the pleasure and duty of them all to put the Drama in order again, and the Master of the Drama in his place—at the head of all.

(8) ¶ And who is this Master, and what his duties?

He is the best man.

Now the best man at Drama must be the best man at Theatres and at playing with Theatricals.

At one period he is *Molière*, the actor-writer. At another time *Sophocles*, dancer-actor-writer. At a third time *Andreini*, actor only. At a fourth time *Shakespeare*, actor-writer. In each period you see the best man was actor. They say that Molière was not a good actor;—what they mean I do not know: that Shakespeare was not a great actor, acted only minor parts: . . . maybe. These two were in a theatre—each in ONE theatre only: . . . did not pop from one to another company; gave time and nature a chance to develop—grew like plants—flowered—bore fruit. . . .

All these men thought in terms of the stage—lived theatre—brought man, mountains, passions, sun, light, dreams, ghosts, into the Theatre: not only by means of words—by any means they could contrive—and to the end of time this will be so and may be so.

And should it happen some day that one who has the actor's talent should be architect (as was Albergati in 1480 and Ariosti in 1530), he may combine his two talents towards creating Drama, and in his own way—yes, even breaking little traditions. It is permitted.

Should he be actor or painter and writer, he too may use these three talents to create Drama . . . and a fourth if he possess it. But no one who is not primarily actor can quite hope to create Drama.

This is what I mean when I speak of the Master of Drama being man of the Theatre.

Another can write plays—these can be often excellent, as 'She Stoops to Conquer' is excellent, or as 'On ne badine pas avec l'amour'; but they have not the genuine touch of the true-bred Dramatist.[1]

Never would I hold that a painter or a writer can be true Dramatist—using their powers over Design and over Words—and these alone. Never *have* I held so. Always have I been misrepresented as holding these views.

I have heard even one great play-writer publicly saying that I am a painter, . . . and that my scenes are all I am thinking of.

---

[1] Exceptions will never cease to prove the rule and so we have in Goldoni, in Rossini, and a few others, men who make us stage pieces which seem made by actors.

(13)

I have made scenes—this is because I see a need,—and possess a talent, for making the Place or Scene in which Drama has to move.

But I have been actor—and I am primarily that: I am able to write a little. I consider no time lost which is spent towards qualifying as a master (though maybe only a little master) of the Theatre—and thus, maybe, of Drama. So much as apology for my shortcomings.

(9) ¶ And here we will go on to consider what are the duties of a Master of the Drama and Theatre.

They are to-day, to recognize that the Theatre as work-place—its stage, scene, actors, and other assistants, is an unwieldy, untidy, and unpractical affair at best, and (I think) to set to work first to simplify it, and then re-elaborate it, and both with the utmost caution.

To simplify an affair of this kind time is necessary. It cannot be done in a month—nor in ten months; maybe not even in ten years.

And to simplify it you must first come to know it so well that as you eliminate you do not reject an essential part of the machine.

To simplify the stage has been the work I have devoted myself to for the last twenty-five years.

I think I have done what I set out to do.[1]

Whether there remains time for me to do what further I had in view remains to be seen.

Now, what I simplified was not merely bits of scenery, and lighting effects, rags of costume and incidental Music.

I simplified the possibilities of Drama.

No scene that I worked at was worked at for its own sake. I thought solely of the movement of the Drama . . . of the actors . . . of the dramatic moments, . . . those long, slow movements and those 'flashes of

---

[1] To simplify the stage:—by this I do not mean stage machinery, or stage scenery, or stage lighting. I mean the whole business of the stage from its actors and scenes down to its very programmes or cloak-rooms. *That* is the Stage:— *nothing less is.* No one *part* concerns me more than another *part.* Each in due time must be put in its right place for the machine to function again.

And when I have set my scene—even taken some years to set it—I have still to bring it to my actors and my actors must learn how to use it.—Made for them, it deserves a like deference and sympathy from them. They cannot be merely 'let loose' in it . . . any more than they could be let loose to speak verse as though it were prose. To *let loose* any one part of this machine is to ruin the machine. No single wheel must be out of place . . . not a bolt missing . . . not a rivet loose. And to see that the whole is in order and keeps in order before the work commences and every moment while it is being done, *the master of this dramatic ship must be in sole command.* This will come to be understood. At present I see that it is not understood.

(14)

lightning' (Coleridge). I saw as I progressed that *things* can, and therefore should, play their parts as well as people: that they combine with the actor and plead for the actor to use them, as the chairs in Molière's plays testify. Not merely are they three or four dead chairs which he placed on the centre of the stage. Yet writers call on us to regard the emptiness of his stage—merely three chairs, they say. Are they mad, these men? Don't they know how Molière made these chairs act—how they are *alive*, and working in combination with the actors?

The chairs and tables in modern plays of which the great Italian actress complains are dead,—there may be six more or sixteen more, or six less; all is as it was . . . dead scene . . . a curse to actors and acting.

A so-called 'real' room is what we present on a stage to-day, . . . real and yet quite dead— expressionless—unable to act.

Molière's chairs, tables, properties of all kinds, were few; he had learned from Italy that they had to be few to be heard—and each of them had to speak at the right moment.

Shakespeare's properties could speak too—although Cromwell and his puritans tore out their tongues and almost dehumanized the whole Shakespearian drama for us.

The tradition once lost, it has never quite recovered its original force.

¶ So, then, to create a simplified stage is the first duty of a master of the Drama.

Not by rejecting electricity because of its defects: not by returning to tallow candles: not by returning to masks: by *avoidance* of nothing, by *returning* to nothing,—but by this process . . .

By reviewing all the Theatrical things known of or once known of as serviceable to the stage, . . . testing them in private, and rejecting those which seem hollow and useless, and retaining all those which stand the test.

What test?—the test whether or no they are capable of expression. That and little else. We must ask ourselves—

Does a wax candle serve us to express the rising sun?—If yes, then use it. Does it not serve?—then reject it. But test it first—pooh-pooh nothing till you've tested it. Does a mask serve us to express such and such a human emotion? If it does, use it;—if not, away with it. Does chanting serve any purpose?—if so, what purpose?—is it of value?—then retain chanting: if none, away with it. Does this or that system of gesture serve?—preserve it—or be done with it. Can actors be taught?— to what extent? Which form of stage is the right one for such and such a play—which next best, which least good. Choose the best. Does it not exist? then build one. Whatever the answers, abide by them. These and a hundred other notions—hopes—fears—have all to be tested to

(15)

simplify that machine known as the Theatre.[1] This will prove very expensive you may fancy. Fancy is not to be relied on, fact is more sure—and fact shows us that to avoid testing everything is the most expensive method of all.

¶ But now consider.—Suppose a mask should be good here—bad there. Good in a Shaw play—bad in a Sophocles play—immense in a new form of play—and rather good in Ibsen.

I ask you to *suppose* this.

Well, then, we will have to both reject and accept the *Mask*;—and this discovery leads us to see that there is *nothing* we can utterly reject. We must accept *all, but not wholly accept*. It also leads us to realize that it is not entire acceptance or entire rejection which we have to go in for, but ordering—development—growth. I repeat it is like a growth, our Theatre.

We have only to put our stages once more in order, to fit all the parts

---

[1] But what I demand and what the Art demands and what the People of a Nation who pay for the Theatres have a right to demand is, that the master of the stage be the sole voice to impose authority . . . and that decisions as to what shall be shall not be voiced by any number of casual warders of the stage, but only by the master of the stage . . . yes, not even by the mistress.

I defy you to create a work of art in the Theatre when any but one mind, and one voice, dominates.

' You will arouse the Socialists and the Communists by *that* speech,' said a friend.

But I know the Socialists and Communists as well as my friend. I have (and doubtless you have) found that all artists who are Communists or Socialists are fierce opponents of a division of authority. For them more than for any one else there must be one boss only.—In fact I begin to think those gentlemen who are supposed to be so disorderly have really just as good an idea of order as Peter of Russia once had . . . better I will not say.

My own idea of order is not a scrap like the Tzar's or the Communists'. My idea is the old one, not my own. If you have 100 men working under you, or if you have 1,000, employ them all the time. Give time to discovering the one job that each can do best. Give him that job. It is the one he will enjoy. The men and women working to-day in theatres are not all doing what they enjoy. They love the theatre, that we must grant—but they do not all love their special job. When I have a theatre I intend to find out what else an actor can do well and if he can do it better than he can act, and if he like to do it he shall be released from acting and set to do that which he enjoys. Thus he will be able to make a great name whereas before (as actor) he could but fail. Of lazy people I will not speak—or concern myself—with them, nor with triflers. They can wake up within a month or go. When I have a theatre I do not intend to enter it armed with a machine-made plan as to how everything is to be done. For as I say, I am no Tzar or Communist. The Theatre is like a garden—things must grow in it according to the laws of nature aided by the small skill of the gardeners.

(16)

of six jig-saw puzzles together which have somehow got confusedly into *one box*, and we can then say we are *ready* to serve the Public.

Now, if you have any notion of organization you will know that this is not to be done in a hurry (except by a Reformer)—or finished on paper with pens and ink, though it can be begun that way. I have begun it for twenty-five years. What I have begun can only be completed in schools under my direction devoted to the examination of this vast material and by men devoted to and conversant with the different branches of the Dramatic art of all lands.

It cannot be begun by one man and be taken up and carried into practice by another without losing practically all its value. It cannot be done that way. The development of an idea or a plan, to be of value, must be completed under the supervision of the originator. This seems not yet to be quite sufficiently understood in these days.

¶ The Master of the Theatre and Drama, having simplified his plan, has now to decide which way he shall take to deliver the goods to the people.

There are two ways. The old way and the new way.

The old way (I still hope it is the youngest) is to put all his discoveries at the service of some Ruler[1]—or rulers;—(Patron was the old and respected title).

This man or these men will see to it that these discoveries go out to the people to be a benefit to them. Such men have existed—but not very often. They more often hamper the master of the Theatre and impose on him their weighty and unimportant Egoisms. This is fatal because it costs too much. Then there is the new way. That is plain *business*.

And, sorry though I am to have to admit it, it seems to me to be the best.

Business need not spoil art;—it has no rights over it—to change it: it is not the business man's affair to change the art; it is the artist's. If he state his position clearly at the start, and if he refuse to accept conditions which are bad for the art, sensible men of business will understand and comply.

But if they do not, he still need not spoil his art, for he can be business man after he has completed his work of art.

So then the Master of the Theatre as an Art has his next task clear before him.

It is to take it to the people unaided.—And there are ways of doing this which only show themselves to us after we have established our name, our right to recognition as first in our line.

To be *First* in this line to hold the Goods is to be master of the Stage.

---

[1] 'Signor Mussolini paid a visit to Madame Eleonora Duse and discussed with her the best means of making the Italian Theatre represent the spiritual life of the nation.'—*Daily Journal*, Dec. 4, 1922.

(17)

D

(10) ¶ Thus far our inquiry into the progress of Scene has shown us that there have been four distinct periods. . . .

It brings us now to a fifth period.

And what a period.

It is the period of internationalism—every kind of scene is 'on the market'.

We must accept it—and simplify as I have said.

Useless were it to go a tour round the eight or nine thousand theatres which exist to-day calling on the managers to reform.

I was never a reformer . . . but some managers are. They have done very much to reform their houses. Some are justly celebrated for instituting reforms. Stanislawsky—Reinhardt—Rouché—Copeau—Barker—Gessner—Antoine—Scandiani, and men before these; . . . Irving, the Duke of Meiningen, Barnay, Talma, and a dozen more. All have been reformers.

But that is all so much to their personal credit as managers: it is never to be placed to the account of the artists. It is a matter of purpose and reveals a capacity to scrub.

Artists who have the creative instinct never reform things, . . . they create them. Reform to them seems a waste of time. Why waste ten hours untangling a tangle of string when in five minutes the artist can make a new ball of string?

And now with your permission I will come to the fifth scene—a scene I have created.[1]

¶ This scene of which I will speak is not the scene shown in the nineteen designs reproduced in this book. But it sprang from these designs.

As this book is not to be issued in a popular edition—as it will go only to those who already know my other books and have had time to study them—I shall not attempt to explain these designs any more than you would ask a musician to 'explain' a fugue he had composed.— I made them in 1907 while I was writing my book 'On the Art of the Theatre', that book which contains the essay 'The Actor and the Übermarionette' and 'The Artists of the Theatre of the Future'.

This much I can add. These designs are all ONE scene, not twenty scenes :—one scene. Not stage scenes made of canvas and wood and artificially lighted by footlights and battens and spot-lights. They are lighted by the sun. They are real, not mechanical.

¶ Had it been thought worth while supporting me after 1900 and 1904,

---

[1] I made this scene (it has been called 'The Thousand Scenes in one Scene') for my own stage.

I am not, alas, a purveyor of sceneries for other people:

I find I am not.

when I produced my first London work on a stage—managing, designing, and rehearsing five complete productions for London, I should by now have made you in actuality the scene here shown in the pictures. I am very sorry I am able to offer so little when I wanted so much to give you much, . . . everything. It is nobody's fault except mine and yours. Mine, that I was not born a Russian or a Spaniard, yours that you have been taught to fail your artists. You cannot help it,—all things are unchangeable and are right as they are, and everywhere in Europe and America this teaching to neglect home-made goods is forced upon mankind. Someone else must explain why. Italians were once taught not to support their Marconis; we in England were the first to aid him. Darwin brings Englishmen a quite simple discovery—which he merely advances as a theory; instantly every one is taught to tear it to pieces tooth and nail. Wagner comes with his hands full of fine things and is rejected by Germany; Nietzsche in German opens prophetic mouth; at once a mailed fist is crammed down his throat. To reject Byron and accept Wordsworth—Southey, was very expensive to the nation. In round figures it cost nearly a crown. To persecute Voltaire and cosset Beaumarchais cost more than one franc—more than eighty millions— it cost the life of the *ancien régime*. To reject wholesale the genuine and to accept the false without any consideration, as is done to-day, is ill-advised.

The error is to go to either extreme, even about the genuine—for then the burden finally returns to the Nation and the people are the losers. Some middle course were better.

¶ So then I would have given you the thing itself, not its likeness, had I been employed after having shown what I could do.

But even in spite of all this indifference I have been able to take the work a step forward towards reality by taking it a step back.

In this way. These etchings we can call the parent work from which another has sprung. This other is smaller—aims to do less—asks less— and in some ways resembles its parent. It was a by-product of the twenty designs at the end of the book.

This lesser scene, 'The Thousand Scenes in one Scene', I have used once in a Theatre in Moscow for a performance of 'Hamlet',[1] and it has

---

[1] Shakespeare and most poetic Drama to be performed has the utmost need of a scene of a special nature . . . a scene with a mobile face.

If careful inquiry is made it will be seen that Shakespeare has not yet had a special scene made for his plays.

I have attempted to supply one—a scene for the poetic Drama, deal it with what it may.

It has often been said, and it will be said again, that Shakespeare creates his

been used by **W. B.** Yeats, to whom I was proud to give it, in some performances in his old Abbey Theatre.

But though it has been used in all, I suppose, for about five hundred performances, it has never been used as I intended it to be used, except on two large model stages which I built in Florence.

On these stages I allowed it to live and it behaved well. In Moscow and Dublin it was not quite free to be itself, and I cannot think it did well.

For this Scene has a life of its own. . . . Not a life which in any way at all runs counter to the life of the Drama. I made it to serve the Drama, and it does so; it serves the whole poetic Drama: and maybe I shall later discover that it can make itself even more useful.

I call it the fifth Scene, for it meets the requirements demanded by the modern spirit—the spirit of incessant *change*: the sceneries we have been using for plays for centuries were merely the old stationary sceneries made to alter. That is quite a different thing to a scene which has a changeable nature.

This scene also has what I call a face. This face expresses.—Its shape receives the light, and in as much as the light changes its position and makes certain other changes, and inasmuch as the scene itself alters its position—the two acting in concert as in a duet, figuring it out together as in a dance—insomuch does it express all the emotions I wish it to express. Always aware that as a background to drama, or to acting, it can but perform its offices with discretion (and I hope I am artist enough to know how to do that), while now and again it can advance and act a somewhat more prominent part.

So much, no more.

I hope it is not too little or too much.

(11) ¶ It is not necessary to lower a curtain during the play for it to pass from scene one to scene two and on to three and to reach scene sixteen.

The scene stands by itself—and is monotone. All the colour used is produced by light, and I use a very great deal of colour now and

---

own scenes as he proceeds, using words to conjure these up before our imagination.

But then he also uses words to conjure up before us the people—their costumes—all. Are we to refuse to visualize all?

Are we to keep Shakespeare for reading silently in our rooms? If so, then he is no longer for a stage and all is well. But if he be performed by actors, not merely by words, and costumed in actual costumes which indicate some period—then let us put a scene round these which shall suggest some place.—Either all words, or let all be visualized.

This is surely the logical conclusion of the whole question.

(20)

again,—such colour as no palette ever can produce. I think I may say that I have not seen colour so rich used in any scene on any stage but this. . . .

I state these few facts because the nineteen black and white designs of the parent scene in this book may mislead you into supposing that I begin and end with white, grey, and black.

¶ This, then, is the fifth scene—a scene of form and colour without any *paint* at all—without any drawing on it—scene simplified, with mobility added to it.

Now for a word on this word 'simplified': . . . let me explain what I mean by it.

The world once used reed pens—then quill pens—and then steel pens. These they dipped into bottles of ink: many times would a man dip his pen into the ink before he could write a page of his letter.

Some one then invented the fountain pen. A man can write his whole letter without dipping his pen once into any bottle.

The world then invented the typewriting machine.

I would liken my scene to the fountain pen and not to the type-writing machine.

It is not a piece of mechanism; it is a simple device, shaped like screens—angular—plain.

Why is it shaped as it is?—why plain, flat screens or walls?

I will tell you. You must suppose me to be doing in front of you rapidly what it took me many years to do slowly. Suppose me, then, searching to find the essential form of the habitation of man, so as to afterwards make a stage habitation for the stage man.

I make rapidly 250 models of his various habitations all over the earth. I make two as used by him 5000 B.C., three 2000 B.C., five 500 B.C., ten 100 B.C., twenty 100 A.D., thirty 1000 A.D., sixty 1500 A.D., fifty 1700 A.D., and seventy 1900 A.D.

I put them up in a line:—I study them.

I intend to reject every piece of each habitation which I do not find in all the others.

Why?

In order to discover which pieces every man since the year one has found essential.

Why?

So as to make *one* scene.

Why?

Because this scene-making is something of an art and not a toy factory.

I do not want the litter of the nursery in my theatre.

(21)

I do not want to waste yearly thousands of pounds on the usual bric-à-brac found in the modern theatre.

Because it is a waste of money—wood—canvas, and I do not want to waste the spectator's powers and temper as spectator and the artist's powers as artist. The artist is to speak to spectators through scene, he is not to display a large doll's house for them.

Having rejected in the two hundred and fifty models any piece which cannot be found in every other piece, I find I am then left with the essential parts which form the habitation of man. The walls remain:

The floor.

The ceiling . . . nothing else.

And how are these shaped?

Are there pillars on them, near them?—do parts protrude—the roof, for example?—some cornice—some skirting? Are there doors, windows, kerbs, and so forth? No. Because I found no such things in all the models. I found that the only things in every habitation of man were flat floor—flat walls—flat roof.

The flat roof is the only part of the human habitation which began at once to vary.

¶ So now you see how it is that my screens, my SCENE, is composed as it is of plain flat walls. I wished to reduce scene to its essentials and I found it reduced itself. I have but done as ordered.

I then added mobility to it.

Why?

First because it seemed to demand it. Secondly because it continued to demand it. It demanded it on behalf of the actor. This mobility allows him to move in a differently shaped scene each night for as long as he wish. Suppose he does not feel at home in this shape, he can change it and rechange it. It is like a hundred pairs of gloves—he can soon find a pair to fit and please him.

Being a device and not an actual habitation, it seemed to ask that I should so make it that it could *seem* now to be the inside and now the outside of any habitation ever known in the world—mud hut or temple, —Palais de Versailles or Mr. Harrod's shop.

And can it be these four places?

It can *seem* like all four . . . . it can seem like four hundred other places. It has a quite clear resemblance to four hundred different places.

I do not mean to say that I shall always show you the wall-paper that is in Mr. Harrod's office . . . or always the gilding in Versailles Palace— or always the marble in the Temple or the mud in the hut . . . But I will give you the form of the four places, the light belonging to each— and three or four details—here a door added—here a grille and here an

(22)

alcove which, when you see them, shall somehow bring up to your mind the conviction that you see what I intend you to see.

And suppose I don't see what you intend me to see? you ask.

There will be thirty out of eighty who do not see as the other fifty see :—that I cannot help . . . that has always been so.

Some people going to see Irving as Mathias in 'The Bells', or Coquelin as M. Jourdain, saw Mathias and saw M. Jourdain. Some fewer number of people did not see any such thing;—they merely saw M. Coquelin and Irving. But if, like every real good playgoer, you go to the Theatre to see what we want to show you, you will see it if we are real good Theatre workers.

What does the device do? you ask.

How does it act?

It does this: it turns in part or whole to receive the play of light.[1]

I would sum up the whole matter in these words.

—Then it is all a matter of the light?

Let us not be in too great a hurry with our 'all a matter of'—I am afraid I cannot say that it is *all* a matter of any *one* thing.

Simplicity and elaboration are not arrived at by any quicker process than that by which a perfect runner or a perfect swimmer achieves the simplification and elaboration necessary to outstrip the others . . . and with the runner and swimmer it is not all a matter of this or that . . . it is a matter of attending to a hundred things all the time.

¶ Let us go on. In creating a scene for a Drama which is worth hearing and worth seeing, we have never to forget what the spectators require.

One of the first of their demands is that they shall be able to see and hear the actor as he performs before us, especially his face (or mask)—and his hands and person.

Therefore any theory which attempts to state the uses of light in relation to scene without stating the use of light to the acting is valueless.[2]

Here then are a few general facts which it is useful to remember.

1. You can see a face—a hand—a vase—a statue better when it is backed by a flat plain non-coloured surface than when backed by something on which a coloured pattern or some other object is painted or carved.

*   *   *

---

[1] It has nothing whatever to do with painting:—what is painted in ancient sceneries I paint with light: there is no paint at all used.

[2] Actor and scene being one, they are to be kept as one before us, or we shall be looking at two things and so lose the value of both. Their value lies in being one.

Being one, the Play, Actor, Scene, has to be kept before us and seen and heard as one—or we shall look from one to another and lose the whole.

(23)

2. The shadow of a thing (face, hand, or statue) is visible to the eye without difficulty or distraction, and is visible at the same time as is the thing itself.

* * *

3. When the face, hand, or statue is removed, a plain screen is a dull thing to look at—the eye tires.

* * *

4. The eye cannot look at two objects at the same time. When we listen to a speaker, be it in a room or in a Hall or in a Theatre, we look at one thing only—his face.

* * *

5. In a Theatre our eyes follow the speaker; therefore when two are speaking it is usual and it is best for these two to be as near one another as possible.

* * *

6. It is essential they shall be in sympathy in their work. Any division in this and we shall at once feel the division and see neither of the actors—our thoughts will wander to the scenery.

* * *

white backcloth

7. The screen against which an actor is best seen is a white one—for it can be shaded to any tone of grey, blackened by shade; coloured any colour, and that without changing the colour of the actor's face, hands, or figure.

* * *

8. There is no need at all for any actor's face to be cast into shadow and the expression lost until it loses distinction of expression . . . then, indeed, it seems best to blot it out.

* * *

9. There was never any need of scenery to take an overdue prominence until the day when the actor lost his power of expression, his power to act, and until he began to resent the right uses of scene and light.

* * *

10. The use of light to the actor is that it will aid him and collaborate with him if he will show it consideration. For light can be used in many dramatic ways—it is for the actor to come to know at least fifty or eighty of these ways. At present he acknowledges about six.

* * *

light can be actor's best friend.

11. The use of light to the actor is only to be studied by the actor

(24)

if he will observe the way light plays its subtle part in real life. If he will observe he will soon come to realize that stage lighting can be his best friend in his work. As an aid to his observation the treatise by Leonardo da Vinci on light can help an actor sufficiently advanced in his studies.

* *

¶ Having stated some of the uses of light to the actor, I can now proceed to state the relation of light to this scene.

The scene turns to receive the play of light.

These two, scene and light, are, as I have said, like two dancers or two singers who are in perfect accord.

The scene supplies the simplest form made up of right angles and flat walls and the light runs in and out and all over them.

The scene is not merely put up (though it stands on its own feet, by the way) on the stage without thought of *how* it be placed and some light turned on without considering *what* light—whence it comes—and what it sets out to do.

In the *placing* of the scene, and in the *turning* to receive the light, and in the *placing* and *directing* of the light lie the little difficulties.

Again, the relation of light to this scene is akin to that of the bow to the violin, or of the pen to the paper.

For the light *travels* over the scene—it does not ever stay in one fixed place, . . . travelling it produces the music. During the whole course of the Drama the light either caresses or cuts,—it floods or it trickles down,—it is never quite still though often enough its movement is not to be detected until an Act has come to an end, when, should we have any power of observation left (and Drama should cure us of any furtive desire to observe), we find our light has changed entirely.

Scene and light then move.

I may have any number of pieces in my scene and I may have any number of lamps.

For the moment we will speak of a scene with five pieces—five screens and of ten lamps.

Having rehearsed a small set of these on my model stage in my room, I come to my Theatre and my larger screens and lamps. I place my screens in their first position. I now pass each screen through its drill— that is to say, my eight or ten manipulators of the screens will practise each screen to see that it is flexible and each man in trim. That done, I myself go to my switchboard and test each tap, each lamp—the force of the light—the smoothness of each pulley, wheel, groove, and so on. . . .

When I am well assured that my screens and my lamps are quite ready, I commence the rehearsal.

The text is read at the pace at which it will be delivered, and at each appointed cue a single or a double leaf of my screen moves—at the same time one of my lamps will begin to play its light at a given strength and from a given position and in a given direction.

At each cue another leaf or other leaves turn—advance—recede—fold up or unfold—imperceptibly, or maybe on some occasions markedly, while at the same time other lamps will begin to function, move their position, change their strengths, alter their direction.[1]

My screens can pass from and to any spot on the stage floor and nothing obstructs their passage.

My light can pass from and to any position in the air or on the stage and so play upon any spot I require.

How these two simple deeds are performed I will show you, with diagrams making it quite clear, the year after I have shown you their performance in several plays.[2]

I regret very much that I cannot show them to you here and now . . . but were I to do so my lighting and its simple device would be quickly caught up by some ever-ready theatre manager or one of his assistants, who would put the thing before you in a manner which I think might satisfy the groundlings to whom Shakespeare alludes, but which I am sure would not satisfy you.

So this is one of those devices which I shall keep for you until we are allowed a theatre—you to come into as spectator, I to work in 'at your service' as artist.

---

[1] This art I can teach you, but not in a hurry, for it has taken me years to come at it.

It requires that you learn the nature of this scene . . . the way it can turn and the way it cannot—its possibilities—its limitations. It requires that you learn the best position for the light, be it sun or electric light; the best means of playing this light upon the scene, colouring it, controlling it. I know of no one who has learnt this yet, although quite a few pretend to the knowledge.

This is what I can teach, for it is what I experiment with daily, so as to teach myself.

I can give you no theories on the scene, for I know as little about it theoretically as the clown in the play knew about the asp which he brought to Cleopatra. On women he theorized, on the worm he refrained; all he said was so much warning:—'Look you,' says he, 'the worm is not to be trusted, but in the keeping of wise people'; yet he goes as I go, saying, 'I wish you joy of the worm.'

[2] After this small scene of screens with its little method of lighting is adopted, I will pass on to the developing of this larger scene shown to you in the twenty etchings. That is a far more difficult undertaking—but to ask to see it put in practice while the smaller version of *something* like the same thing remains to be carried out for the English Theatre—and in a theatre of my own—is, I think, looking a little too far ahead.

It is enough to add that I can light the face, hands, and person of any given actor, be he in any part of the stage, and without lighting the scene, and I can paint with light any part of the scene without obliterating the actor for a moment.

And I could not say that eight years ago.

I am enabled to say so now because I have discovered how to do this in the course of the last four years.

The further question, whether it is desirable and necessary *always* to light the actor at every moment of the play with the same quantity of light is one which I to-day believe may have to be gone into *with* the actor . . . no one is more reasonable than he when the theatre is open and running smoothly.

¶ A little more is to be said and I am done.

I can colour my screens or the actor's form to a great extent in the same degree and with the same strength and quality as a painter uses on his canvas. I employ only light . . . he employs his paints.

I am limited by my medium as he is by his, and both of us have to obey our particular tools and materials.—He cannot do anything beyond paint on a flat surface in colours—I can do no more than project my light on to my screens and figures.

But whereas he had his materials and tools discovered for him and a method of long-standing taught him, I have had to find out my materials and tools, and I have been obliged to invent a method for using them.

Therefore, if I have not yet reached as perfect a method of using these things as he has, and if I cannot reach it before I am obliged to give up the work, others to whom I shall leave my plans and experiments must continue on after I have done and discover better ways if they can.

It is for this serious reason, so as to preserve, so as not to lose what discoveries I have made, that I very much hope I shall have a workshop and enough assistants who can carry on this work after my death. To no others will I entrust what I hope I am not too presumptuous in considering of value.

This page remains as a testimony that I announced my need of these things and that I was given the means to preserve my discoveries for those who come after me.

Or it may serve as a testimony to the contrary.

GORDON CRAIG.

1 9 2 2

(27)

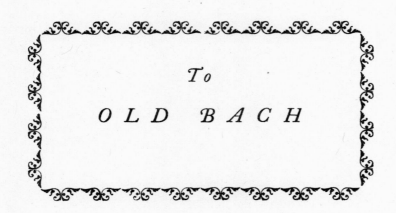

To

OLD BACH

Plate 1

1907

Plate 2

1907

Plate 3

1907

Plate 4

1907

Plate 5

1907

Plate 6

1907

Plate 7

1907

Plate 8

1907

Plate 9

1907

Plate 10

1907

Plate 11

Plate 12

1907

Plate 13

1907

Plate 14

1907

Plate 15

Plate 16

1907

Plate 17

1907

Plate 18

1911

Plate 19

1907